DATE DUE	
	JUN 25 2011		

SOUTH AMERICA TODAY

SURINAME

ATLANTIC OCEAN

6°N

Nieuw Amsterdam

• Nieuw Nickerie

Paramaribo ✪

GUYANA

Albina
•

Kwakoegron
•

Coppename River

Brokopondo
•

FRENCH
GUIANA
(France)

Van Blommestein
Lake

Suriname River

Maroni River

SURINAME

4°N

WILHELMINA MOUNTAINS

Courantyne River

Cottica
•

Tapanahoni River

N
W   E
S

Litani River

2°N

BRAZIL

0   50   100 Miles
0   50   100 Kilometers
Oblique Conic Conformal Projection

58°W   56°W   54°W

SOUTH AMERICA TODAY

SURINAME

Colleen Madonna Flood Williams

Mason Crest Publishers
Philadelphia

Produced by OTTN Publishing, Stockton, N.J.

Mason Crest Publishers
370 Reed Road
Broomall, PA 19008
www.masoncrest.com

First printing

1 3 5 7 9 8 6 4 2

Library of Congress Cataloging-in-Publication Data

Williams, Colleen Madonna Flood.
  Suriname / Colleen Madonna Flood Williams.
      p. cm. — (South America today)
  Includes index.
  ISBN 978-1-4222-0641-6 (hardcover) — ISBN 978-1-4222-0708-6 (pbk.)
  1. Suriname—Juvenile literature. [1. Suriname.] I. Title.
  F2408.5.W55 2008
  988.3—dc22

                                    2008032319

SOUTH AMERICA
TODAY

Argentina

Bolivia

Brazil

Chile

Colombia

South America:
Facts & Figures

Ecuador

Guyana

Paraguay

Peru

Suriname

Uruguay

Venezuela

Table of Contents

Discovering South America

James D. Henderson

South America is a cornucopia of natural resources, a treasure house of ecological variety. It is also a continent of striking human diversity and geographic extremes. Yet in spite of that, most South Americans share a set of cultural similarities. Most of the continent's inhabitants are properly termed "Latin" Americans. This means that they speak a Romance language (one closely related to Latin), particularly Spanish or Portuguese. It means, too, that most practice Roman Catholicism and share the Mediterranean cultural patterns brought by the Spanish and Portuguese who settled the continent over five centuries ago.

Still, it is never hard to spot departures from these cultural norms. Bolivia, Peru, and Ecuador, for example, have significant Indian populations who speak their own languages and follow their own customs. In Paraguay the main Indian language, Guaraní, is accepted as official along with Spanish. Nor are all South Americans Catholics. Today Protestantism is making steady gains, while in Brazil many citizens practice African religions right along with Catholicism and Protestantism.

South America is a lightly populated continent, having just 6 percent of the world's people. It is also the world's most tropical continent, for a larger percentage of its land falls between the tropics of Cancer and Capricorn than is the case with any other continent. The world's driest desert is there, the Atacama in northern Chile, where no one has ever seen a drop of rain fall. And the world's wettest place is there too, the Chocó region of Colombia, along that country's border with Panama. There it rains almost every day. South America also has some of the world's highest mountains, the Andes,

A fisherman in his canoe on the Tapanoholi River.

and its greatest river, the Amazon.

So welcome to South America! Through this colorfully illustrated series of books you will travel through 12 countries, from giant Brazil to small Suriname. On your way you will learn about the geography, the history, the economy, and the people of each one. Geared to the needs of teachers and students, each volume contains book and web sources for further study, a chronology, project and report ideas, and even recipes of tasty and easy-to-prepare dishes popular in the countries studied. Each volume describes the country's national holidays and the cities and towns where they are held. And each book is indexed.

You are embarking on a voyage of discovery that will take you to lands not so far away, but as interesting and exotic as any in the world.

(Opposite) A Djuka man fishes with a bow and arrow in the waters of Granholosoela Falls, located above Poketi. (Right) Members of Suriname's Tirio tribe point to their village on the first map made of their rain forest territory.

1 The Land

ON THE NORTHEASTERN coast of South America, nestled between Guyana to the west, French Guiana to the east, and Brazil to the south, sits a little-known country called the Republic of Suriname. It is a small nation, covering slightly more area than the state of Georgia. The population of Suriname is slightly smaller than that of Denver, Colorado.

Suriname is unique in several respects. It developed as a Dutch colony on a continent dominated by Spanish and Portuguese colonial influence. It is also the youngest nation in South America, having gained independence as recently as 1975. And despite its small size, Suriname has one of the world's largest nature preserves—the Central Suriname Nature Reserve, established in 1998.

Suriname is made up primarily of tropical rain forests, coastal swampland, a few mountain ranges, and some gradually sloping hills. The country's limited coastal area is fairly level.

Most of Suriname's cities have been built along flat, muddy coastal areas. City planners decided on these locations because much of the rest of the country is so thickly forested that it could be reached only by airplane or riverboat. Approximately 80 percent of Suriname is covered by tropical rain forest. (In fact, the country contains more rain forest than all the nations of Central America put together.)

Three Regions

Suriname can be divided into three major regions. Each one runs from east to west, somewhat parallel to the coastline of the nation. They are the coastal plain; the central region, which consists of grassland and tropical rain forest; and the southern region, characterized by heavily forested mountains, hills, and *savannas*.

The coastal region is about 226 miles (364 kilometers) long, with a depth from about 62 miles (100 km) in the west to 19 miles (30 km) in the east. Much of this area is covered with mudflats. Along the coastline, there are also marshes and mangrove swamps. There are few sandy beaches along Suriname's Atlantic shores.

Inland from the Atlantic coastline lies a low flat area called the New Coastal Plain. The New Coastal Plain includes approximately 6,600 square miles (17,000 sq km) of land. Almost all of this land is swampland.

South of this area is the Old Coastal Plain. The Old Coastal Plain often

A child searches for gold in a river near Brokopondo. Suriname has untapped resources of gold and other minerals. However, environmental pollution has resulted from mining and industry in the country.

rises as high as 40 feet (12 meters) above sea level. This plain covers about 1,550 square miles (4,013 sq km). It is primarily swamps, sand ridges, and clay flats.

Inland from the Old Coastal Plain is the Zanderij formation, in the central region. This section of Suriname, which is 40 miles (64 km) wide, is

Quick Facts: The Geography of Suriname

Location: northern South America, bordering the Atlantic Ocean, between French Guiana and Guyana

Area: (slightly larger than the U.S. state of Georgia)
   total: 63,039 square miles (163,270 sq km)
   land: 62,344 square miles (161,470 sq km)
   water: 695 square miles (1,800 sq km)

Borders: Brazil, 371 miles (597 km); French Guiana, 317 miles (510 km); Guyana, 373 miles (600 km)

Climate: tropical; moderated by trade winds

Terrain: mostly rolling hills; narrow coastal plain with swamps

Elevation extremes:
   lowest point: unnamed location in the coastal plain—7 feet (2 meters) below sea level
   highest point: Juliana Top—4,035 feet (1,230 meters)

Natural hazards: seasonal flooding during the rainy season between December and April

Source: Adapted from CIA World Factbook 2002.

made up of rolling hills that are covered by the dense plant life of the tropical rain forest. Along the Zanderij formation, swamps and savanna can also be found. The savanna is a flat grassland dotted occasionally with trees.

The land that makes up the central region was formed upon white sand deposits. The soil in the region is very rich in quartz. It is also rich in *bauxite*, an ore used to manufacture aluminum.

Suriname's southern region is famous for its dense Amazonian rain forests. The natural vegetation here is composed primarily of tropical trees and plants. Occasionally, marshes extend outward from creeks and rivers that run through the rain forest.

The southern region also includes a central mountain range with a few thickly forested hilly areas. The highest mountain peak, at 4,035 feet (1,230 meters), is Juliana Top. This peak is part of Suriname's largest mountain range, the Wilhelmina Mountains.

Major Waterways

The region that includes the modern nations of Suriname, Guyana, and French Guiana was once called Guiana, or "land of waters," by the ancient *Amerindians* who lived there. The natives chose this name because of the many rivers and streams in this South American region.

Suriname's major rivers flow northward into the Atlantic Ocean. The Courantyne (or Corantijn) River forms part of Suriname's boundary with Guyana. The Maroni (or Marowijne) River forms part of the nation's border with French Guiana. The Coppename and Suriname are the other major rivers, and Suriname has many other streams and rivers flowing through it.

The Climate

Suriname has a tropical climate. The nation's temperatures range from 73°F to 90°F (22°C to 32°C). The most brutal weather condition that the Surinamese people face is called the *sibibusi* ("bush sweeping" or "forest broom"), a driving, pouring rain.

In Suriname, the four seasons are determined by the presence or absence of rainfall. A short dry season runs from February to April, followed by a long rainy season running from April to August. The months between August and December are the long dry season, and the months between December and February are the short rainy season.

The coastal area of Suriname receives the most rainfall. This region sees over 80 inches (203 centimeters) of rainfall per year. In the interior region of Suriname, approximately 60 inches (152 cm) of rain falls each year. The hottest month is September and the wettest month is June.

Nature Reserves and Parks

Unlike the coasts of many other Latin American countries, the coasts of Suriname are not covered with sandy beaches to attract tourists. However, the coasts are covered with birds. Suriname is an important rest stop for more than 20 species of wading birds and provides a safe haven for several kinds of turtles. Five of Suriname's 12 protected areas are found along its coast. These are designed to protect bird and turtle habitats.

Marshes and mangrove swamps can be found all along the coastline. The mudflats, marshes, and mangrove swamps provide a rich feeding ground for hundreds of thousands of wading birds. Many of these birds migrate here from North America. Bird-watchers from all over the world flock to Suriname. They come to observe the coastal wading birds. Egrets, scarlet ibises, and pelicans can be seen feeding in different areas along Suriname's lush shores.

There are a few sandy spots along the coast. Turtles, not tourists, seem to take the greatest advantage of these beaches. Some of these sandy shores can be found at the Galibi Reserve. This reserve is near the Maroni *estuary* in

A young three-toed sloth hangs from treetop branches near Paramaribo.

northeast Suriname. Leatherbacks, green turtles, olive ridleys, and other types of marine turtles nest along these shores. The olive ridley turtle population that nests at Galibi is the largest recorded one in the Western Atlantic region. The leatherback turtle population that nests here is also one of the largest in the world. National laws protect all the species of sea turtles that nest in Suriname.

The plants and animals of the Central Refuge are also well protected. The jaguar, giant armadillo, giant river otter, tapir, and 400 bird species are native to this region. Eight different species of monkeys also coexist in the

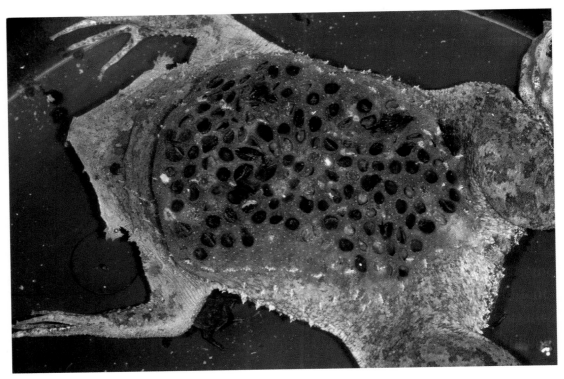

One of the strange creatures native only to Suriname is the Suriname toad. It is unusual because female toads carry fertilized eggs on their backs. The toad's skin grows over the eggs to protect them until they hatch.

Central Refuge's forests. They are unafraid of humans and have never had reason to fear hunters.

The Sipaliwini Savanna is located along the headwaters of the Sipaliwini River. To its south and east, the Sipaliwini grassland borders Brazil. Across its terrain, groups of Mauritia palm trees huddle together, creating shady resting spots for humans and animals alike. It is also a designated wildlife reserve. More than 300 species of birds have been observed on the Sipaliwini Savanna. There are more sightings of the sun parakeet and the peach-fronted parakeet here than anywhere else in the world. Giant anteaters, blue poison arrow frogs, and many other animals share this refuge with the birds.

Other nature reserves and parks located in Suriname include Hertenrits, Coppename Monding, Wia-Wia, Brinckheuvel, Boven Coesewijne, Copi, Wane Kreek, Peruvia, and Brownsberg Nature Park.

(Opposite) A cannon and Dutch military buildings from the 18th century at the Zeelandia Fort, Suriname. In 1667 the Netherlands traded control of the Suriname area to the British in exchange for the Dutch settlement of New Amsterdam—modern-day New York. (Right) Jules Wijdenbosch served as president of Suriname from 1996 to 2000.

2 A Turbulent History

THE FIRST PEOPLE TO live in the land that today is Suriname were Amerindians. About 10,000 years ago these people moved into the open Sipaliwini Savanna, where they lived as hunters and gatherers. They hunted large prehistoric animals and gathered fruits, nuts, and other plants. They used simple stone tools and moved from place to place, following the movements of herds of mammoth and mastodon. They are known as the Surinen Indians, and it is from them that the nation of Suriname gets its name.

Five thousand years later, the native people of Suriname still lived a nomadic lifestyle. However, they were moving less often and for a different reason. The great herds of mastodon and mammoth had disappeared. To survive, the people had become farmers. They planted arrowroot, yucca, sweet potatoes, peanuts, cotton, and tobacco, and supplemented their agricultural diets with fish and small game. When they moved, it was to search for better farmland when the soil in one area had been depleted.

Because they no longer needed to move so often, these natives of Suriname had time to learn new skills. They become adept at making clay pottery, stone jewelry, and cotton aprons. They carved large dugout canoes. The natives also became proficient fishermen. Some even learned to navigate the ocean as well as the rivers of the rain forest.

Eventually, the Surinen Indians were displaced by two other native groups from South America, the Arawaks and the Caribs. These two tribes soon began to battle over territory in Suriname. Many of the more peaceful Arawak people fled to the islands of the Caribbean to avoid fighting against the fierce Caribs. However, both groups still held territory in the country at the end of the 15th century.

The Arrival of Europeans

Carib and Arawak territories in Suriname were soon to be claimed by another group—the Europeans. The Spanish made the first claim on the land; in 1593 a *conquistador* named Domingo de Vera took possession of the area for Spain. The Portuguese, who had settled in Brazil to the south, also claimed the region (then called Guiana) as theirs. And by 1602 explorers and adventurers from Holland began to settle in Suriname. Between 1620 and 1640, the French and English established outposts in Guiana as well.

In 1651 a group of English farmers came to the region from the island of Barbados. They established plantations that produced sugar, cotton, and coffee. Within a few years, the English farmers had established a profitable colony of more than 500 sugar plantations. The English were soon joined by a small group of Portuguese Jews. The Jewish colonists were fleeing religious persecution that they had encountered in Brazil. Together, the English farmers and Jewish businessmen and laborers worked together to ensure that their colony prospered.

Meanwhile, the Netherlands and England went to war several times over control of the surrounding seas. Their first war lasted from 1652 to 1654, the second from 1665 to 1667. The two countries ended the second war by signing the Treaty of Breda. As a result of the agreement, the Dutch gave up their colony at New Amsterdam (the settlement that today is New York City) to the English. In return, England gave its lands in South America to the Dutch. The region that today is Suriname became a Dutch colony, and was called Dutch Guiana.

The Colonial Era

The Dutch restricted colonization to the coastal region, because the rain forests were strange and dangerous. Because Holland, like Dutch Guiana, has many low coastal plains, the Dutch settlers were able to create a good farm system. They drained waters to create *polders*, and they built *dikes* and *seawalls* with *floodgates* to control the ocean and rivers and reclaim fertile lands. To irrigate their crops and drain their fields, they built canals. They also started coffee and sugarcane plantations, and brought slaves over from Africa to work them.

Despite their expertise at farming on low coastal plains, the Dutch could not so easily overcome the other problems that they encountered. Pirates attacked the settlements, and sometimes their African slaves escaped into the rain forest, where they formed their own tribes. These escaped slaves managed to survive in the jungles; the Dutch called them *Maroons*.

This engraving shows armed slaves during a rebellion in Suriname, circa 1832. The Dutch brought Africans to South America to work on coffee and sugarcane plantations. Slavery persisted in the region until the 1870s.

The Dutch still needed slaves to work the land. They tried to follow the escaped Maroons into the forests and recapture them. Usually the Dutch were not successful, though when they were, they often cut the hamstring muscles of the slaves' legs so they could not run away again. Dutch cruelty was well known throughout the other colonies in South America and the Caribbean.

Refusing to endure the injustice of slavery, the slaves began to rebel. The Maroons sometimes helped, waging devastating surprise attacks against the settlers. In 1767 the Dutch signed peace treaties with three groups of Maroons. The Maroons agreed not to help slave rebellions, and to return future runaway slaves. In exchange, the Dutch allowed the Maroons to live in their society as freedmen.

The Netherlands eventually abolished slavery in 1863. However, according to the law, slaves had to remain on their plantations for 10 years. They were paid very meager wages during this time. In

These corn husk dolls were made by the descendants of African slaves on Suriname.

1873 many slaves left the plantations. As a result, the owners faced a worker shortage, and to keep the plantations operating, they brought in workers from other countries. Most of these workers were *indentured servants* who agreed to work for a number of years on the plantation. In exchange, the owner paid the cost of their ship passage to Dutch Guiana and gave them food and lodging. Over the next 70 years, tens of thousands of indentured servants came from the Dutch East Indies (Indonesia), India, China, Portugal, and Lebanon.

By the 1940s, the economy of Dutch Guiana was changing. The sugar plantations were no longer the backbone of the economy. New products were in greater demand: rubber, gold, and a mineral called bauxite. Alcoa, an American company, had become interested in Dutch Guiana's rich deposits of bauxite ore after World War I, which ended in 1918. The company began mining for this ore in the eastern region of Dutch Guiana. The processing of bauxite and the production of aluminum were in full swing by 1941.

During World War II, the construction of new U.S. airplanes called for large quantities of aluminum, which Dutch Guiana supplied to the United States. The swell in industry helped the economy of Dutch Guiana as well as the American war effort.

Moving Toward Independence

After the Second World War ended in 1945, many people in Dutch Guiana began demanding that the Netherlands give them independence. In 1949 the Dutch government gave new rights to the people of the country. By 1954 the Netherlands had relinquished control of most of Dutch Guiana's internal affairs, although the Netherlands maintained control over foreign affairs and defense policies.

In 1973 a *Creole* man named Henck Arron was elected prime minister of Dutch Guiana. Arron had promised to work for Dutch Guiana's complete independence from the Netherlands. After his election, Arron almost immediately began negotiating with the Netherlands to gain complete freedom for the country.

Within two years, Arron had fulfilled his promise. The Netherlands agreed to grant the colony total independence. It also pledged financial support to the tiny new country, agreeing to give its former colony approximately $100 million per year over the next 10 years.

Dutch Guiana officially became the Republic of Suriname on November 25, 1975. Dr. Johan Ferrier became the country's first president. Henck Arron retained his title of prime minister.

Growing Pains

Financial aid from the Netherlands, as well as from the United States, did not seem to be enough to help Suriname. Almost one-third of the new nation's population moved to the Netherlands because they were afraid the country would collapse. Many of the emigrants were affluent business-people, who took with them not only their families, but also their money and valuable business know-how. To make things worse, the demand for bauxite fell and Suriname's economy began to flounder. Workers went on strike and unemployment rose.

In 1980 a violent military coup took place. For the next two years, the country had no prime minister. Henk Chin A. Sen served as president, although he was only a figurehead. A military leader named Desi Bouterse was really in control of Suriname, and he was not afraid to use violence to get his own way. The government arrested and executed 15 citizens for protesting the leadership and demanding a return to a constitutional government.

The United States protested against the Bouterse government by refusing to send Suriname any further economic aid. The Netherlands also suspended financial aid to Suriname.

The country remained turbulent throughout the 1980s. In 1986 a group called the Surinamese Liberation Army (SLA) began violently assaulting industrial targets. The SLA hoped to restore constitutional order through its guerrilla war. Within months, the SLA had caused many bauxite mines and refineries to shut down.

A new constitution was put into place in 1987, and the next year Ramsewak Shankar was elected president. However, Bouterse and his military still exercised great power within Suriname.

President Shankar worked to reach a peaceful agreement with the SLA. In 1989 the two sides agreed to end the violence. Bouterse did not agree with the peace accord and vowed to keep fighting the SLA, and so the violence continued. In 1990 Bouterse initiated a plot to oust Shankar from office that proved successful.

After Ronald Venetiaan was elected president in 1991, he was able to reduce the influence of Bouterse on the national government. He also negotiated a peace agreement with the SLA in 1992.

In 1996 Bouterse's friend and ally Jules Wijdenbosch was elected

Two members of a Surinamese organization, Collective Resistance, lower their country's flag to half-mast after occupying Suriname's embassy in The Hague, 1984. Collective Resistance supported striking workers in Suriname's bauxite mines and processing factories. For most of the 1980s internal tensions between citizens and the government divided Suriname.

Desi Bouterse campaigns for president in Paramaribo, February 2000. A military and political leader, Bouterse has been perhaps the most powerful person in Suriname for more than two decades.

president. The next year the Dutch government issued an international arrest warrant for Bouterse. The warrant accused him of smuggling more than two tons of cocaine into the Netherlands. In defiance, Wijdenbosch appointed Bouterse Advisor of State and refused to *extradite* Bouterse to the Netherlands. In 1999 the Dutch government tried Bouterse *in absentia* and convicted him of drug smuggling.

By this time, however, the people of Suriname had grown very unhappy with their government. There were widespread riots and protests throughout the country. To restore order, the government decided to hold elections a year early, in 2000. Ronald Venetiaan was once again elected president. In response to these efforts toward democracy, both the Netherlands and the United States started to give aid to Suriname once again. This financial assistance has greatly helped the national economy.

However, not everyone is happy about Venetiaan's presidency. He allowed companies from North America and Asia to mine gold and clear timber in the country, hoping that the foreign companies would provide work for unemployed Surinamese citizens and boost the country's economy. This policy caused great concern among environmental groups. They feared that uncaring corporations would spoil the traditional homes of Suriname's Maroons and Amerindians, as well as destroy its rain forests.

The May 2005 presidential election demonstrated the dissatisfaction many Surinamese felt with their government. Venetiaan's party gained the most votes, but not the two-thirds majority needed for reelection. After two separate votes, neither he nor his opponent from Desi Bouterse's party achieved the majority. Local and national assemblies voted Venetiaan back into office in August 2005, ending months of political tension.

(Opposite) Barges of bauxite ore arrive at the Suralco refinery. Bauxite is a key element in aluminum production.
(Right) All of South America's leaders (including Suriname's Ronald Venetiaan, third from left) met in August 2000 to discuss regional immigration during the Summit of South American Presidents in Brasília.

3 A Struggling Economy

ACCORDING TO THE World Bank, in the year 2000 Suriname was the 17th-richest nation in the world in terms of natural resources. Within its borders Suriname has untapped fortunes in gold, manganese, uranium, iron ore, nickel, and platinum.

With a new government in place, and new economic plans taking shape, Suriname's economy is ripe for change. Undoubtedly, this change will be in part due to the continued oil exploration that is taking place onshore as well as offshore. The offshore seismic exploration for oil and drilling started in May 1992. Because of the regional geology of Suriname, geologists believe that the country has great potential for oil production.

Industrial Sector

The industrial sector is made up of construction, manufacturing, energy, mining, and fish-processing businesses, which employ approximately 14 percent of the labor force in Suriname.

Suriname is one of the largest producers of bauxite in the world. Most of this bauxite is processed locally into aluminum. Suriname's economy has been very dependent upon its bauxite industry since the early 1940s. A great deal of the bauxite mining takes place along the coastal plain at Moengo. Paranam, a locale in the hills southeast of Paramaribo, is another major bauxite mining and processing area.

A forklift loads aluminum ingots, which will be shipped to Europe. Aluminum and related products account for approximately three-quarters of the value of Suriname's annual exports. The Suriname Aluminum Company (Suralco), which operates a large alumina refinery and aluminum smelter in Paranam, is a subsidiary of the Aluminum Company of America (Alcoa).

Quick Facts: The Economy of Suriname

Gross domestic product (GDP*):
$4.1 billion (purchasing power parity) (2005 est.)

GDP per capita: $7,800

Inflation: 6.4%

Natural resources: timber, hydropower, fish, kaolin, shrimp, bauxite, gold, and small amounts of nickel, copper, platinum, iron ore

Agriculture (10.8% of GDP): paddy rice, bananas, palm kernels, coconuts, plantains, peanuts, beef, chickens, shrimp, forest products (2005 est.)

Industry (24.4% of GDP): bauxite and gold mining, alumina production, oil, lumbering, food processing, fishing

Services (64.8% of GDP): tourism, telecommunications services, government services (2005 est.)

Foreign trade (2006 est.):

Exports—$1.39 billion: alumina, gold, crude oil, lumber, shrimp and fish, rice, bananas

Imports—$1.30 billion: capital equipment, petroleum, iron and steel products, agricultural products, consumer goods.

Currency exchange rate:
2.745 Surinamese dollars = U.S. $1 (August 2008)

* GDP or gross domestic product = the total value of goods and services produced in a year. All figures are 2007 estimates unless otherwise indicated. Sources: CIA World Factbook 2008; International Monetary Fund; Bloomberg.com

The *alumina* and aluminum businesses require a great deal of energy. In the 1960s, Alcoa built a $150 million dam near Afobaka. The company built this dam to produce cheap hydroelectric energy for its alumina and aluminum businesses. This dam created a 600-square-mile (1,553-sq-km) body of water called W. J. van Blommestein Lake. It is one of the largest artificial lakes in the world.

Workers in Suriname are free to join independent trade unions. The unions have an active and fairly powerful voice in national politics.

Eco-tourism has become popular with many visitors to Latin America, and Suriname has many features to offer tourists. The Kumalu eco-resort, a simple area with eight thatch and wood huts similar to native dwellings, occupies a small island in the Pikien River, a tributary of the Suriname River.

Collective bargaining—negotiations between the union and company management about pay and working conditions—is also legal.

Agricultural Sector

Rice is Suriname's basic food staple. It is also the agricultural sector's biggest export. Not only do many people in Suriname work every day to produce rice for the tables of others, they put it on their own tables as well.

The agricultural sector employs about 8 percent of the Surinamese labor force. The main food crops produced are rice, sugarcane, bananas, and coconuts. The most important meat products are chicken, beef, veal, pork, duck, and mutton. After rice, shrimp is Suriname's largest food export.

Service Sector

Suriname's service sector employs almost 80 percent of its labor force. It also contributes about 65 percent of the nation's gross domestic product (GDP). This important business sector includes telecommunications services, transportation services, and tourism services, among others.

One growing service industry in Suriname is *eco-tourism*. The present government supports and promotes this expanding business. Suriname offers eco-tourists opportunities for white-water rafting, photography, fishing, bird-watching, nature hikes, adventure trips, and interaction with Maroon and Amerindian cultures. Surinamese hotel, bar, and restaurant workers all profit from an increase in the eco-tourism industry.

Living Below the Poverty Line

Relatively few Americans can conceive of living below the poverty line. The poverty line in Suriname is defined as living in a household with subsistence-level conditions and a monthly income of $50 per adult. (In other words, if you are a child living with both of your parents and fall under the poverty line, your household income would be less than $100 per month.) Today 70 percent of Surinamese families live below that poverty line.

(Opposite) A woman trims a cassava cake with a leaf as it cooks on a griddle. (Right) A Djuka man and boy watch an elderly man weaving a basket. The baskets are used as fire fans, for storage, and as cassava strainers and presses.

4 The People and Culture

THE POPULATION OF Suriname is like a cultural bowl of soup. The Dutch provide the broth, or the base flavor, of this soup. As in any good soup, however, each added ingredient brings to the soup its own distinct flavor. The other ethnic ingredients of Suriname's cultural soup include the Maroons and Amerindians in the interior, and the Creoles, Hindustanis, Javanese, Chinese, and Europeans in the coastal zone.

The official language in Suriname is Dutch, but English is widely spoken here. The *lingua franca* is called "Sranang Tongo." This is the less formal language that the Surinamese people use to communicate with each other. A great variety of other languages are spoken here as well. Some of these include Hindi, Javanese, and Chinese.

Quick Facts: The People of Suriname

Population: 475,996

Ethnic groups: Hindustani (also known locally as East Indians), 37%; Creole (mixed white and black), 31%; Javanese, 15%; Maroons, 10%; Amerindian, 2%; Chinese, 2%; white, 1%; other, 2%

Age structure:
0–14 years: 27.5%
15–64 years: 66.2%
65 years and over: 6.3%

Population growth rate: 1.1%

Birth rate: 17.02 births/1,000 population

Death rate: 5.51 deaths/1,000 population

Infant mortality rate: 19.45 deaths/ 1,000 live births

Life expectancy at birth:
total population: 73.48 years
male: 70.76 years
female: 76.39 years

Total fertility rate: 2.01 children born per woman

Religions: Hindu, 27.4%; Muslim, 19.6%; Roman Catholic, 22.8%; Protestant (predominantly Moravian), 25.2%; indigenous beliefs, about 5%.

Languages: Dutch is the official language, and English is widely spoken. Sranang Tongo (sometimes called Taki-Taki), is the native language of Creoles and much of the younger population and is *lingua franca* among others. Hindustani (a dialect of Hindi) and Javanese are also spoken.

Literacy rate (age 15 and older): 89.6% (2004 est.)

*All figures are 2008 estimates unless otherwise noted.
Source: CIA World Factbook 2008.

The Maroon and Amerindian Population

The Arawaks, Caribs, Tirios, and Wajanas are four of Suriname's remaining Amerindian tribes. The six Maroon groups in Suriname are the descendants of runaway African slaves. These tribes are the Djuka, Saramaka, Matuwari, Paramaccaner, Aluku, and Quinti. Within each tribe are Opo Maroons, who live on the upper parts of the rivers, and Bilo

Maroons, who live on the lower parts of the rivers. For the most part, they are friendly to each other and to the Amerindians of the bush.

The Tirios live in the south of Suriname. Three of their larger villages are named Apetina, Tepu, and Kwamalasamutu. In the Tirio-dominated village of Kwamalasamutu, there are over 1,000 residents. The Wajanas live along the Tapanahoni, Lawa, and Paru Rivers of Suriname, Brazil, and French Guiana.

The Arawaks and Caribs are lowland Amerindians. They live in villages built on the savannas and along the rivers south of Paramaribo. They can also be found living in settlements along the lower Maroni River, in the Coppename Basin near the Courantyne River, and beside the Nickerie River.

Education

Dutch is the official language of instruction in Surinamese schools, though it is seldom spoken outside of school. Because many families speak the language of their family of origin at home and in their day-to-day lives, learning Dutch is a challenge for many students.

Two Creole girls from Suriname wear the *anjisa*, a traditional head covering, in a photo from the 1950s. These head coverings could be starched and folded in various styles to indicate the mood of the wearer.

English is also taught for two to three hours a week at the secondary school level and beyond. This is part of the reason why so many Surinamese people at least understand, if not speak, English. Spanish instruction is available on an elective basis at the secondary school level.

There are both public and private religious schools in Suriname. The school year runs from October to mid-August. By law, a Surinamese child must attend school from age 6 until age 12. In the cities this law is enforced; however, in the rural areas it often is not.

Children attend primary school until they reach the age of 12. Those who wish to continue their studies attend junior secondary school until the age of 16. Some students attend vocational school after finishing primary school.

From age 16 to 18, students may attend senior secondary school. In some ways this is similar to a high school in the United States. However, students can attend different schools, depending on the results of their entrance exams. Some students attend academic schools in preparation for college, while others attend vocational schools to gain job skills.

Higher education is provided by the University of Suriname, the Institute for Advanced Training of Teachers, or the Academy for Higher Art and Culture. The University of Suriname has three departments, or faculties: the Faculty of Social Sciences, the Faculty of Technological Science and Agricultural Sciences, and the Faculty of Medical Sciences.

The Arts

The arts are a part of daily Surinamese life. Cooking, clothing, and carvings are all a part of Suriname's diverse multicultural heritage. There are many different ethnic forms of music and dance in Suriname, too.

On the streets of Paramaribo, musicians play and dancers dance for all to enjoy. Here, the melodies of a *guqin*, or Chinese zither, might float through the air. Javanese music, played by what is called a **gamelan** orchestra, is just as likely to be heard. Javanese storytelling dancers, dressed in elaborate costumes, may accompany a gamelan orchestra and share an ancient tale.

Kaseko is the dance music of the Surinamese Creoles. It is a mix of Western march music, jazz, calypso, and other popular music from the countries surrounding Suriname. Like Javanese music, *Kaseko* will get people dancing in the streets, though it is usually not as formal an event as a Javanese storytelling dance.

Far from the city streets, the

A Tirio Indian poses in Suriname. This native is apprenticed to a shaman; one day he will be the tribe's healer and religious leader.

Caribs or Galibis have their own form of dancing. To initiate a shaman, they perform a religious ceremonial dance called the *Marakka*.

Cassava cakes are made for special ceremonies and for less formal occasions. The Saramaka Maroons eat these cakes regularly, although they make them with designs so intricate that they can be considered works of art. The Maroon women draw the designs on the surface of the cakes with their fingers. Many of the cakes' decorations have special symbolic meanings.

While the Maroons eat beautiful works of art, the Javanese wear beautiful works of art. Much of their clothing is made from batik cloth. Roughly translated, the word *batik* is Javanese for "dots." Batik clothing is made by drawing patterns on both sides of a cloth with molten wax. Next, the cloth is soaked in a dye-bath. The wax-free areas are saturated with color. The wax is then removed. This process is repeated using different-colored dyes to create a multicolored batik design on the cloth.

Many Surinamese men and women practice the art of carving, too. Women take *calabash*, a kind of gourd, and carve the shells into spoons, bowls, and other household items. Men use forest hardwoods to carve tools, canoe paddles, and gifts for the women in their lives. The better the carver, the more intricate his or her designs become, though most carved items still remain useful in daily living activities. Art truly is a part of daily life in Suriname!

The Pastimes

Soccer is the most popular sport in Suriname, as it is in most other South American nations. People also entertain themselves by playing tennis, basketball, and golf. Other favorite activities include swimming in public pools and sailing.

Many Surinamese practice judo and the other martial arts. They do so for the purposes of personal defense, fun, and their own fitness. The martial arts were brought here by immigrants from Asia.

Cyber cafés are becoming more and more popular in Suriname. In Paramaribo there are several cyber cafés and other places that provide access to the Internet for a fee. At most of these places those who wish Internet access are charged by the half hour.

Two men navigate their dugout canoe through rapids on a river in Suriname. Most of Suriname's population lives along the coast; approximately 80 percent of the country is wilderness and rain forest.

Hindu women offer flowers in the Courantyne River during a celebration in Nieuw Nickerie. More than a quarter of Suriname's people follow Hindu beliefs; most Hindus are descendants of the East Indians who came to the country as laborers in the late 19th century.

Religion

Christianity, Hinduism, and Islam are all practiced in Suriname. The Roman Catholic and Moravian churches also have a visible presence in this South American nation. Most ethnic groups of Suriname focus on appreciating and preserving their own language, culture, and religion.

The Surinamese Constitution provides for freedom of religion, and the government has respected this right. The people of Suriname have, also. How else could one explain a Jewish synagogue in Paramaribo existing peacefully next to a Muslim mosque?

One favorite festival, Phagwa (also called Holi), is a Hindu tradition. This festival celebrates the beginning of spring. People throw perfumes, scented powders, and fragrant oils at each other while reciting mantras. As they do this, they shout *Sub Holy*, a phrase wishing another good luck.

The religious tolerance of Suriname helps to explain how the music styles of the Quinti, Njuka, Saramaka, and other groups have survived without hindrance from the government or missionaries. Some Maroon traditions, like Santería and voodoo, center on the performance of songs and dances of the neo-African tradition. The African words used to accompany these songs and dances often seek to invoke spirit possession.

Two views of Paramaribo, the capital of Suriname. (Opposite) Dutch housing from the late 17th century lines a street. (Right) A 19th-century painting of the city and its harbor. Today Paramaribo, the largest city in Suriname, is home to more than 200,000 people.

5 Cities and Communities

SURINAME IS DIVIDED into 10 political districts. These include Paramaribo (on the left bank of the Suriname River); Wanica (south and west of Paramaribo); Para (a mining and forestry area of central Suriname); Brokopondo (a reservoir area with large-scale agriculture); Commewijne (a farming area on the right bank of the Suriname River); Saramacca (a traditional area of small farms and fishing with modern rice and banana farms); Coronie (a populated coastal area with coconut and rice farms); Nickerie (a populated coastal area in the northwest); Marowijne (a populated part of northeastern Suriname); and Sipaliwini (a region of dense rain forest).

The capital of Suriname and the largest city is Paramaribo, located on the

The quiet streets of downtown Fort Zeelandia. A fort originally built in the area by French settlers was later captured and strengthened by the British, who called it Fort Willoughby. The fort was captured by the Dutch in 1667. The buildings around the original fortification are military quarters dating from the 1790s and heavily influenced by Dutch colonial architectural styles.

west bank of the Suriname River. It is home to more than 200,000 inhabitants. One of the most interesting places in Paramaribo is the old city center, home to the presidential palace. This building was built in the first half of the 18th century. The building and its beautiful private garden are only open to the public on November 25, Suriname's Independence Day.

Along the *Waterkant*, or Waterside Boulevard, ferries travel across the Suriname River to the village of Meerzorg. People rush in and out of Paramaribo's central market—housed in a tall white building—carrying food, clothing, and other items.

African, Indian, Chinese, and European merchants all gather at the market to sell their wares. Some sell jewelry, and others sell carvings. The majority of merchants here sell food, including fresh fruit and dried spices.

On any given day, the market is alive with the sights, sounds, and smells of Suriname.

The second-largest city is Lelydorp, located in Wanica. The city is also a district capital and has a population of about 17,000. The road that runs between Paramaribo and Lelydorp used to be called Pad van Wanica, "the path to Wanica." In 1984 it was renamed Indira Gandhi weg in honor of the assassinated prime minister of India, Indira Gandhi.

Lelydorp has experienced a name change, too. Lelydorp was originally called Kofi-Djompo, but was then renamed after the Dutch engineer Cornelis Lely, who was governor of Suriname from 1903 to 1905.

Nieuw Nickerie, in Nickerie, is Suriname's third-largest city and is home to more than 13,000 Surinamese. Nieuw Nickerie is located at the western end of Suriname's East-West Highway, and a ferry runs between the city and Guyana.

One interesting fact about Nieuw Nickerie is that the entire city has been moved—not once, but twice! The city used to be on the west bank of the Courantyne River. It is now located on the east bank of the river, Suriname's western border. The city had to be moved in 1870, and then again in 1879, because of erosion. To prevent the need for another move, the city had a protective seawall built alongside the river.

Suriname's cities and communities all seem to be quite adept at adapting to change: changes in government, changes in location, changes in industry. But while many things continue to change in Suriname, the smallest nation in South America the country's cultural diversity remains a constant.

A Calendar of Surinamese Festivals

January

On January 1, the people celebrate **New Year's Day**. This is considered a national holiday.

February

February 25 is observed as **Day of the Revolution**.

May

On May 1, **Labor Day** is observed.

July

July 1 is **Emancipation Day** or "Keti Koti"—one of the most important holidays in Suriname. Keti Koti (translated as "break chains") celebrates the day the Dutch slave owners set their slaves free.

November

On November 25, the people of Suriname celebrate **Independence Day**, which marks the establishment of the Republic of Suriname.

December

On December 25, people in Suriname observe **Christmas**. The next day, December 26, is **Boxing Day**. Though this festival is of English origin, it is observed as a national holiday in Suriname.

Religious Observances

Hindu, Muslim, Christian, and Jewish residents of Suriname all observe a number of important holy days related to their religions. Some of these are on particular days each year (for example, Christmas, which occurs each year on December 25, is the Christian celebration of the birth of Jesus Christ). However, many other major celebrations occur according to a lunar calendar, in which the months are related to the phases of the moon. A lunar month is shorter than the typical month of the Gregorian, or Western, calendar (28 days for the lunar calendar, compared with 30 or 31 days for the Gregorian calendar). Therefore, the festival dates vary from year to year. Other celebrations are observed seasonally.

There are several major festivals observed by Hindus in Suriname. The four-day festival of **Divali**, which occurs in October or November at the end of the harvest season, is marked by the lighting of many lamps; some people set off fireworks also. Special meals are common and people generally stay up late to enjoy this joyous celebration. The third day of the festival is usually also the celebration of **Padava**, the Hindu New Year.

Another favorite festival is **Phagwa** (also called Holi), which celebrates the beginning of spring. People throw perfumes, scented powders, and fragrant oils at each other while reciting mantras. As they do this, they shout *Sub Holy*, a phrase wishing another good luck.

The most significant month of the Muslim lunar calendar is the ninth month, **Ramadan**. This is a time of sacrifice for devout Muslims. During Ramadan, Muslims are not supposed to eat or drink between sunup and sundown. They are also supposed to restrict their activities during these

A Calendar of Surinamese Festivals

hours to necessary duties, such as going to work. After the sun has set completely, Muslims make a special prayer before eating a small meal.

Ramadan ends with a three-day festival called **Eid al-Fitr**, or "breaking of the fast." During this time families get together and exchange gifts.

The **Eid al-Adha** (Feast of Sacrifice) is a more serious occasion. It takes place at the end of the hajj period, during which Muslims make their way to Mecca on pilgrimage. Eid al-Adha commemorates the willingness of the patriarch Abraham to sacrifice his son to God. In the story, God instead provided a sheep. According to tradition, Muslim families should slaughter and eat a sheep on this day.

The major Christian festivals on the lunar cycle involve the suffering and death of Jesus Christ. **Ash Wednesday** marks the start of a period of self-sacrifice called **Lent**, which lasts for 40 days. The final eight days of Lent are known as Holy Week. A number of important days are observed, including **Palm Sunday**, which commemorates Jesus' arrival in Jerusalem; **Holy Thursday**, which marks the night of the Last Supper; **Good Friday**, the day of Jesus' death on the cross; and **Easter Sunday**, which marks his resurrection. Forty days after Easter Sunday, Christians celebrate the **Feast of the Ascension**, which marks the day the risen Christ returned to Heaven.

The tiny Jewish population of Suriname celebrates all of their important festivals on their ancient lunar calendar. The **High Holy Days** are celebrated during the first 10 days of Tishri, the seventh month in the Jewish calendar. **Rosh Hashanah**, the Jewish New Year, is celebrated during the first two days of Tishri. Special meals are created for family gatherings. The 10th day of Tishri, **Yom Kippur**, is the most solemn day of the Jewish year. Yom Kippur, the Day of Atonement, is a time for devout Jews to fast, pray, and reflect on the previous year.

Other important festivals include **Purim**, which marks an important victory of the ancient Israelites; **Passover**, an eight-day observance that reminds Jews of their escape from slavery in Egypt; **Shauvot**, the Feast of the Weeks, which is held at the start of the harvest season and also commemorates the Ten Commandments given to Moses and the Israelites after they fled from Egypt; and **Hanukkah**, the Festival of Lights, an eight-day festival in honor of the relighting of the sacred flame in the temple of Jerusalem, after it was freed from Greek control by the Maccabees.

Recipes

Surinamese cuisine is an exotic mix of East Indian, Indian, Creole, and Chinese cuisines.

Peanut Soup
1-1/2 cups unsalted roasted peanuts
1 tsp hot pepper sauce
Salt to taste
2 tbsp soy sauce
3 cups chicken stock
1 large onion, finely chopped
1-1/2 cups milk
Croutons

Directions:
1. Mix the peanuts and 1 cup of the chicken stock and puree.
2. In a saucepan, combine the pureed peanuts, remainder of the chicken stock, onion, hot pepper sauce, and salt to taste.
3. Cook over low heat for 15 minutes. Stir occasionally.
4. Stir in the soy sauce and add the milk.
5. Continue cooking over low heat for another 5 minutes.
6. Remove soup from heat.
7. Pour into bowls, garnish with croutons, and serve.

Rice Chicken
1 chicken
1 small onion
1 clove of garlic
1 tsp laos powder of fresh laos
1 tsp ginger powder of fresh ginger
2 tbsp soy sauce
Chicken bouillon cubes
1 tsp cooking oil

Directions:
1. Cut the chicken into small pieces and fry in oil.
2. Add the onion, garlic, and other ingredients.
3. Add the soy sauce and the chicken bouillon cubes, then a little bit of water.
4. Let the chicken cook until well done.
5. Serve with rice and vegetables such as Chinese string beans or *amsoi* (like bok choy).

Bruine Bonen (Brown Beans)

6–8 pieces of chicken (one per person)
1/2 lb salt pork, cubed, skin and extra fat removed
2 hot dogs, cut up
3 tbsp chopped onion
2 chicken bouillon cubes
1 tsp black pepper
1 tsp paprika
1 tbsp ketchup or tomato paste
Two 15-oz cans pinto beans or other brown beans
(can use more beans to stretch the recipe)
5 whole allspice seeds
1/4 cup sugar
5 tbsp oil

Directions:

1. Mix chopped onion, 1 chicken bouillon cube (crushed), black pepper, and 1/2 teaspoon of paprika. Coat the chicken with this mixture and set aside.
2. Boil the salt pork in 1 quart of water for 10–15 minutes. Throw away the water when done.
3. Fry the salt pork in oil until brown, then remove from pan.
4. Wipe the chopped onion off the chicken. Fry the chicken in the same oil for about 10 minutes. Remove from pan.
5. Fry onions in remaining oil until tender.
6. Add ketchup, stir. Return salt pork to pan. Add cut-up hot dogs. Cook for a few more minutes.
7. Empty one can of beans into a 2-quart pot. (Do not drain.) Mash the beans.
8. Add the other can of beans. (Do not mash.) Fill one bean can with water and add.
9. Add the allspice, the other chicken bouillion block, 1/2 teaspoon of paprika, and sugar. Stir.
10. Add all the meat. Clean the frying pan with a little water and add to the pot.
11. Boil over medium heat until chicken is tender.
12. Serve over rice.

Cassava Cake

1 cup raw cassava, grated
1 egg
1/2 cup milk
2-1/2 oz butter
1 cup sugar
3-1/2 tbsp wheat flour
2 tsp baking powder
Salt to taste

Directions:

1. Mix cassava with egg and milk.
2. Beat butter and sugar until creamy.
3. Mix butter and sugar mixture with the cassava, egg, and milk mixture.
4. In a separate bowl, mix together flour, baking powder, and a pinch of salt.
5. Add flour mixture to egg mixture. Mix well.
6. Pour into cake pan and bake for 40 minutes.

Glossary

alumina—aluminum oxide.

Amerindians—American Indians; the indigenous peoples of the Western Hemisphere.

bauxite—an ore used to manufacture aluminum.

calabash—a hard tree fruit of the bignonia (tropical vine) family that is used by Maroon carvers in Suriname and French Guiana to make bowls and other utensils as gifts.

cassava—a tropical plant of the spurge family, having edible starchy roots used for making bread or cakes and cassava cereal.

conquistador—a Spanish conqueror or adventurer in the Americas during the 16th century.

Creole—in Suriname and in the English-speaking Caribbean, this term refers to a person of mixed African and European ancestry. (In Latin America, the term *Creole* denotes someone of European ancestry born in the Western Hemisphere.)

dike—an embankment made of earth or other suitable materials to protect an area of land from an overflow of water or to regulate water flow.

eco-tourism—a kind of tourism geared to the protection and preservation of the environment.

estuary—a water passage where the tide meets a river current.

extradite—to hand over a criminal suspect living in one country to another country in order that the suspect may be tried there.

floodgates—gates constructed to shut out or release the flow of water over spillways of a dam.

Glossary

gamelan—an orchestra that is usually made up of percussion instruments such as bronze and iron gongs, gong chimes, cymbals, bells, and two-headed drums; some gamelan varieties may feature flutes, bowed and plucked strings, or vocalists.

in absentia—in someone's or something's absence.

indentured servant—a person who immigrates to another country and agrees to work for an employer for a set number of years; in return, the employer pays the worker's passage to the country and provides room and board during the term of employment.

lingua franca—any language used as a common tongue among people who speak diverse languages.

Maroons—name given to people who from slavery in Suriname and created their own settlements in the jungles; today, the term is used to mean the descendants of these escaped slaves.

polders—pieces of land below sea level that are surrounded by a dike.

savannas—tropical or subtropical grasslands covered with drought-resistant under-brush and a few trees here and there.

seawalls—offshore structures built to protect a harbor from waves or currents.

sibibusi—a torrential rain that occurs in Suriname.

Project and Report Ideas

Report Ideas

Research and give a report on the life of Jan Matzeliger. Read Barbara Mitchell's book *Shoes for Everyone*, a biography of the half-Dutch/half-black Surinamese man who in the late 19th century invented a machine that revolutionized the shoemaking industry by helping make shoes more sturdy and durable.

Investigate the differences between polders, dikes, and seawalls. Write a report that describes the history and use of each of these. Create illustrations of each to accompany your report.

Project Ideas

- Create a collage that includes symbols of each of Suriname's cultural groups. Present the collage to the rest of the class and explain the symbols.

- Research the architecture of Suriname's capital city, Paramaribo. Draw a typical colonial Paramaribo home and explain to your class what it reveals about architectural history.

- Find out what the Surinamese mean by "Coca-Cola" creeks. Explain to your class just what these are, how they came to be called "Coca-Cola" creeks, what they are composed of, and where they are located.

- Research the sea turtles of Galibi. Create a poster that illustrates the life cycle of a sea turtle.

- Explain the roles of Christopher Columbus, Alonso de Ojeda, and Domingo de Vera in Surinamese history.

- Create a map that shows the locations of several of Suriname's important Maroon and Amerindian villages.

- Organize an eco-tour of Suriname for your classmates. Create several maps of different interesting parts of Suriname. Be sure to include the types of plants and animals that your visitors will see along the way. Also include major land forms and waterways on your maps.

Project and Report Ideas

Politics/Current Events

Stage a talk show featuring several Surinamese politicians discussing the political history of Suriname. With a group of students, research several Surinamese presidents, military leaders, or other political figures. Have each student choose a particular figure and learn about his or her political ideas. Present the talk show to your class. Choose an important event in Surinamese history and let the "professional experts" of the class discuss its political significance.

Chronology

1498	Christopher Columbus sights the coast of Suriname.
1593	Spanish explorers visit the area and name it Surinam, after the country's natives, the Surinen.
1602	The Dutch establish temporary settlements.
1651	The British and their slaves set up the first permanent European settlement in Suriname.
1667	The British trade their part of Suriname to the Netherlands in exchange for New Amsterdam (later called New York City).
1682	Coffee and sugarcane plantations are established; settlers import African slaves to work the plantations.
1799–1802, 1804–16	British rule is imposed once again.
1863	Slavery is abolished; indentured laborers are brought in from India, Java, and China to work on plantations.
1916	Aluminum Company of America (Alcoa) begins mining bauxite, which gradually becomes Suriname's main export.
1954	Suriname is given full autonomy, with the Netherlands retaining control over its defense and foreign affairs.
1975	Suriname becomes independent with Johan Ferrier as president and Henck Arron, of the Suriname National Party (NPS), as prime minister; more than a third of the population immigrates to the Netherlands.
1980	Arron's government is ousted in a military coup, but President Ferrier refuses to recognize the military regime and appoints Henk Chin A. Sen of the Nationalist Republican Party (PNR) to lead a civilian administration; army replaces Ferrier with Chin A. Sen.

1982   Armed forces seize power in a coup led by Lieutenant Colonel Desire (Desi) Bouterse and set up Revolutionary People's Front; 15 opposition leaders are charged with plotting a coup and are executed; the Netherlands and the United States respond by cutting off economic aid.

1986   Surinamese Liberation Army (SLA) begins guerrilla war with the aim of restoring constitutional order; within months principal bauxite mines and refineries are forced to shut down.

1987   Some 97 percent of electorate approves new civilian constitution.

1988   Ramsewak Shankar, a former agriculture minister, is elected president.

1990   Shankar is ousted in military coup masterminded by Bouterse.

1991   Ronald Venetiaan is elected president.

1992   Peace accord is reached with SLA.

1996   Jules Wijdenbosch, an ally of Bouterse, is elected president.

1997   Dutch government issues international arrest warrant for Bouterse on charges of smuggling cocaine into the Netherlands, but Suriname refuses to extradite him.

1999   Dutch court convicts Bouterse for drug smuggling after trying him in absentia.

2000   Venetiaan becomes president, after elections are held early due to widespread protests.

2004   The national currency, the guilder, is overhauled and replaced with the Surinamese dollar.

2005   Venetiaan is re-appointed president after months of uncertainty.

2006   Over 20,000 are left homeless after widespread flooding.

2007   The United Nations resolves conflict between Suriname and Guyana over control of a maritime basin; both countries are granted access to the area.

Further Reading/Internet Resources

Carlin, Eithne B., and Jacques Arends, editors. *Atlas of the Languages of Suriname*. Seattle: University of Washington Press, 2003.

Oostindie, Gert, editor. *Paradise Overseas*. Oxford, UK: Macmillan Education, 2005.

Price, Richard, and Sally Price. *Maroon Arts*. Boston: Beacon Press, 2000.

Sims, Doris J. *Shoes Got Soles: Jan Ernest Matzeliger*. Los Angeles: Children's Cultu-Lit Book Company, 1994.

Westoll, Andrew. *The Riverbones: Stumbling after Eden in the Jungles of Suriname*. Toronto: Emblem Editions, 2008.

Travel Information

http://www.lonelyplanet.com/worldguide/destinations/south-america/suriname
http://www.travel.state.gov/travel/cis_pa_tw/cis/cis_1030.html
http://www.parbo.com/tourism/

Economic and Political Information

https://www.cia.gov/library/publications/the-world-factbook/geos/ns.html
http://pdba.georgetown.edu/Constitutions/Suriname/english.html
http://www.surinam.net/
http://www.state.gov/r/pa/ei/bgn/1893.htm

For More Information

Suriname Tourism Department
Ministry of Transport, Communication and Tourism
Cornelis Jongbawstraat 2
Paramaribo, Suriname
P.O. Box 656, Paramaribo, Suriname
Phone: (+597) 471163 or (+597) 478421
Fax: (+597) 510555
Telex: 292 SURAIR SN

Embassy of the Republic of Suriname
4301 Connecticut Ave., NW
Suite 460
Washington, D.C. 20008
Phone: (202) 244-7488
e-mail: embsur@erols.com

The Consulate of Suriname in Miami
7235 NW 19th St.
Suite A
Miami, FL 33126
Phone: (305) 593-2697

Index

Index/Picture Credits

Contributors

Senior Consulting Editor **James D. Henderson** is professor of international studies at Coastal Carolina University. He is the author of *Conservative Thought in Twentieth Century Latin America: The Ideals of Laureano Gómez* (1988; Spanish edition *Las ideas de Laureano Gómez* published in 1985); *When Colombia Bled: A History of the Violence in Tolima* (1985; Spanish edition *Cuando Colombia se desangró, una historia de la Violencia en metrópoli y provincia,* 1984); and coauthor of *A Reference Guide to Latin American History* (2000) and *Ten Notable Women of Latin America* (1978).

Mr. Henderson earned a bachelor's degree in history from Centenary College of Louisiana, and a master's degree in history from the University of Arizona. He then spent three years in the Peace Corps, serving in Colombia, before earning his doctorate in Latin American history in 1972 at Texas Christian University.

Colleen Madonna Flood Williams resides in Homer, Alaska, with her husband, Paul Williams, son, Dillon Meehan, and their Bouvier des Flandres, Kosmos Kramer. She has a Bachelor's Degree in Elementary Education, with a minor in Art.